Chicken Back

Natasha Hunter

BookLeaf Publishing

India | USA | UK

Presentation by *BookLeaf Publishing*

Web: www.bookleafpub.com

E-mail: info@bookleafpub.com

ISBN: 9789358315028

First edition 2024

This is dedicated to my grandmother Frankie Mae, My father "Billy" and my daughter Aries Moon. May the love the two formers demonstrated to me on this Earth be exponentially bestowed upon you through me, Aries. You're mama's baby.

ACKNOWLEDGEMENT

I'd like to acknowledge the Lord God because he knows what we've talked about many years ago and everything since. Love you.
To my family and friends, who have lent a listening ear, provided valuable insights, and offered solace, thank you. Sometimes your presence means way more than you may think.
To the people that inspired these entries, thank you. I'd like to believe that in most instances we were doing the best that we could, with what we had. In the instances that we weren't, I pray we now have the wisdom and compassion to do better.

PREFACE

As I scour entries in my journal for "Chicken Back," I am acutely aware of the courage it takes to share the intimate details of one's life. I am asking myself, "Are you sure you wanna do this," just as I know it's surely done. This memoir is more than buzzwords and a slick cohesiveness that makes you feel good—it is a raw testament to the resilience of the human spirit and the transformative power of personal growth. Just like the chicken backs on the cover of this book, even the poorest can be transformed and turned into something beautiful and rich!

In these pages, you will find some raw and unfiltered excerpts from my journey—shadows of childhood abuse, instances of not having very high self-worth, and the search for love in the wrong places, people, and things. Each journal entry is a step, a heartbeat, a testament to the strength that emerged from the depths of my struggles.

As I invite you into the recesses of my life through journal entries and reflective notes, I do so with the understanding that our stories, though unique, are cords that create the rope of the human experience. It is my sincerest hope that you find echoes of your desires, understandings, moments of clarity, and resilience in these pages and that, together, we can celebrate the triumph of the human spirit.

To those who may be opening these pages without prior knowledge of my journey, I extend my gratitude. Thank you for allowing me to share my story with you. May it inspire, educate, and above all, remind us all that, no matter the depth of our scars, there is strength in healing and power in resilience.

With heartfelt sincerity,

Natasha Hunter

I knew. 9/6/96

...somebody asked me, "How does it feel to be married?" At first, I said "It's the same," but now almost two hours later I can see I was wrong. Sometimes you go into something thinking you can change the way things are but you can't. That's something I need to learn, I need to learn that the sun's gonna rise, the wind's gonna blow and the grass is going to grow. I have this problem where I think I can handle everything. I think I'm invincible in that I can bounce back from anything, that nothing can phase me because in 24 hours it's a whole new day. But this isn't true... I know there will be times when my husband will make me mad and likewise I him. All I have to learn to do is find myself a place to go when things get bad and bring myself back to the way that things are supposed to be. Maybe that's why I joined the military, my stepfather was very very strict and I guess that's kind of why I feel like I can handle everything that life throws my way because if you live 12 years of your life under some power freak ain't much that can seem worse. I think this also has something to do with my problems with **** I hate when he tells me to do stuff repeatedly or move or don't wear this, don't do that, or do this or do that. But maybe that's why I'm with him—once again testing myself, testing my strengths, and weaknesses, trying to see exactly how much damage was done. Trying to see exactly what effect this man had on my ability to trust people and my ability to forgive.

*So this is one of my first recorded instances of ignoring myself and not understanding the constitution I have over my own body. I want to be clear it wasn't that I didn't want to marry this man, he was the best thing I had known up until this time. What I did know is that I didn't wanna get engaged one day and be married the next day! I knew I wanted to go back to the base with an engagement ring to show off for a minute, but I didn't know how to say that and was scared he would change his mind if I did. If you think you feel a little bad for him, don't, LOL. We remained in touch and years later I asked him,

"If you had no intention of being a husband, why did you marry me?" He responded with " I just didn't want anyone else to have you."

I met a fly guy. 6/15/2004

I met this guy and he was so fly
Did he pull up in a Lexus or a Benz?
I don't know but his gas tank was full of
compliments and he didn't stop in front of his
friends.
Well was he wearing Iceberg or Prada?
Neither, Nada but he was fresh to def with his
convo, far from the same ol' and his smile spoke
before I heard "Hello!"
C'mon least tell me he had on Timbs??
Yeah, you know what I like, but the illest part of
all we really went on a hike!
I thought you had your heels on?
I did, not that kind of hike. We moved through
mountains of lies, and valleys of distrust,
molehills of pride and traversed the thickets that
separate us.
Mmm. Was he blingin'?
The brightest I've eva seen, I was blinded by it, I
thought it might hurt me until he told me to
come closer...
Wow, his chain was blingin' like that?!
Haven't you been listening girl what chain?! I'm
talking about his heart, I'm talking about his
brain.

*This poem is so funny to me. I've always been a bit of a cerebral sista and I love the connections that occur and flow naturally. I'm actually talking about someone I started talking to through BlackPlanet.com

Talkin' shit/Who am I?
Between 6/2004 & 11/2004

... It's OK you can say my name just be sure to enunciate. You see, I can land on the Planet of the Apes, with a handful of grapes, some crepes, and a bag of mix tapes, and by the time they stop rubbing their napes, they'll be eating out of my palm and loving it.

Am I distant? Sometimes, this Earth is not my only residence. Even when I'm still I move, like the lower mantle way down beneath your feet. The Law of Gravity keeps you near. It's strong and I'm deep.

*Still feeling the effects of the BlackPlanet suitor

The man I guess you could call the prototype. Late 2004

Careful... does he dare awaken the slumbering beauty that exists inside of me? If the wonderful colors burst out with the force of glass shattering, would he choose not to know me? The red is hot and lava-like as it winds, and the orange is intense so bright it may blind. I was happy, joyous mood, quite sappy... green is lush, exotic, and smells like thyme, blue is like rain, exotic drops falling in time. Indigo is deep, it is soul and thoughts, violet... well just like the ones you gave me that day, needs no explanation. That day. In every way, I'd like to share my worth, for I believe that is my duty and has been since birth.

*Had me open, didn't he? Well, I'm not mad at it at all. I had never felt so seen and alive. He didn't demand anything of me but to be me and it was EXCITING!

...I'm in love with this man.
11/09/2004

I would...
Hold your hand walking through the park, cozy
up against you when it's dark. Make iced tea
when you're parched and say your name with
my back arched. Sweep the floor, organize your
sock drawer, and fix the handle. Mail the bill
you forgot to pay, pick up your dry cleaning
since I was going that way. Open the cookbook
and try that recipe... make it with olive oil
instead of sesame. There are other ways but I
somehow lost track, I think I stopped at 10 to be
exact...

*...and that's all you get because I was giving PICK-ME at the time, but that's how I felt. I was as ready to love as I ever have been and then...

When it was over—my fault.
6/30/2005

My fantasy escaped me for reality. Watched you fly away on Golden Wings as I walk along the street one foot in the gutter. Sometimes I see your shadow, feel your breath on my neck, smell your scent in the wind and I wait patiently for your essence to feel my soul again. Maybe it's in vain and was never meant to be. For my life is mine and I remain free.

*Bay.Bee. When I say I felt how I hurt that man? Now as I stated in the title, our reason for separating was my fault, and I take full responsibility for that. One to grow on.

8/29/10 Solace

I'm at peace with all of the things that make me
me, as well as what makes you you.
Contradictions, insecurities, and immaturities...
none of us are perfect, yet we find ourselves
being perfect for each other and I suppose there's
a beauty in that.

Repeat offender 09/21/2010

So it's not her I was in love with, he reasoned as he exited her lobby and the wind caused him to stuff his hands quite roughly into his pockets. It was her innocence, her "Golly Gee" as he often referred to it. It seemed to be something the Midwest girls had naturally, he mused, but it always seemed to diminish over time.. after dealing with men like him, the thought finished rather quietly in a recessed corner of his mind. He jumped in the taxi oblivious to the sadness etched on his face.

*Sometimes I wonder if accountability is truly a foreign concept to people, or do they just feign ignorance to avoid it?

1/20/11 The Devil's Tongue

His verbal viscosity coded the right side of my brain with images of the last, first, and next time. Weaving a physical tapestry too complex for text and containing colors so vivid, I can only see them through my blindfold. That nicca knows he can lie, because I still went.

The pain has a B side
1/12/12 & 9/28/13

How do I feel today? I am making progress in my life and I'll be eight months next week it's so... real. The fact that I'm gonna be a mom and I'll be doing it here pretty much alone. Despite what you've shown I still hold hope... believe that you'll come around and play a part in your daughter's life. Not really expecting you to be in mine—not sure I'd even want you to at this point, but I do want you to love her wholeheartedly and give her attention. Bond with her and get to know her.

So it's been a year and eight months since my last journal entry in this notebook. So much has changed yet so much hasn't? Most of the changes have occurred on my side of things but to your credit, you have changed your behavior some. I think the biggest thing for me is just how you behave as though I don't exist. Like Aries was just dropped out of the sky. Don't understand why the sudden rejection, deflection... my therapist says it's because of things in my childhood and not you that I'm

having a hard time "letting go." So I resurrected
this journal to discover that. Here we go...

*This is the first time a therapist made the
connection between my childhood traumas and
my romantic choices. I would be lying if I said
that that recognition has been easy. It hasn't, in
any way shape or form. However, I'm at the
place now where I realize that it was necessary
for my total development as a person and
especially as a mother.

STATION BREAK 12/8/23 technically 12/9 but let me rock!

I'd just like to insert here how proud I am of myself. That is something old me wouldn't say out loud and even less put in print to be here for all eternity because I was taught that you don't praise yourself, you wait for others to do it for you. What a crock! I always said I was gonna write a book and name it Chicken Back, just one of my ultimate turning a negative into positive moments. Here I am doing just that and the little girl in me is just doing the cabbage patch right now! I just wanted to take a minute from this collection and give you that moment to share with me right here. By taking the chance and purchasing my book, you are now a part of my real-life dream. How cool is that? THANK YOU!

More notes from therapy that did not stick at the time.
12/28/2013

1. You cannot heal the wounds left by a person with another person
2. Life changes are hard to do, add a person also going through their separate change, and then add another person who is not in the least of ways self-sufficient and not expected to be.
3. When grieving you need to give yourself time to process, not distractions.

The note that did stick from that same session tho'… 12/28/2013 b-side

Clear communication is a must, especially with yourself. Here's an exercise. Every time you say or hear the word "can't" replace it with "won't" and see how much closer to the truth you are. Now you can make better decisions.

*Do it. A simple way to gain another perspective, and start switching your responses from debilitating thoughts to plans of action.

12/8/13 Understanding what a gift you are and the gifts you have.

It is imperative that you understand that not only are you a gift, you come with gifts. Discover this by being curious and open to experiences that will add to you. It is within these experiences that you will discover how much your wonder and enthusiasm are a gift to those who will pour into you. You stand a better chance of creating reciprocal relationships when you can clearly define who you are and what you offer.

1/31/14

Called to wish him a Happy Birthday and was greeted with "You know as a daughter, I'd give you a C or D." Wow. You can't have a real conversation with avoidants. I'm not sure that they think correctly. Appearing to get it, and truthfully understand what is being said, and after that moment, nothing changes. Stating things like "You can't keep blaming your parents," to avoid discussions about things that I feel affect me as a parent. Is wanting to discuss what happened blaming? Or is it an attempt to reconcile how I arrived at this place? Being upset with me is a false justification for not doing the right thing, the thing that you are scared to do. Be a compassionate human.
*This is one of a few attempts I made to reconcile with my stepfather. There would be more until I allowed myself to have none. It burns the cockles of my heart to know that this is a relationship I can't fix, but the realization freed me to pour into ones that don't need fixin'. These relationships are of my choosing and instead of having to till the ground and get the right chemical balance for growth, (maybe!) these relationships have good soil and are ready for the seed of me to impart something beautiful.

Convincing myself to file child support. 4/3/2014

Because you won't communicate with me as a parent. Because I'm not going to send the message to my daughter that men don't have to be responsible for the people they bring into this world if they don't want to. Because I'm not going to send the message that she should do it all alone just because she can. Regardless of the end state, if we made her, we are going to take care of her.

*Still standing on this, but not focused on this. God provides, Amen?

When I started realizing how I continually played myself.
6/02/2014

It was then that I realized my expectations were the problem. Not that I had them but in who I was expecting to fulfill them. I was expecting unhappy people to be happy for me and with me. Why did I expect people who felt they could only rely on themselves to do anything for me?

Meaningless vapors
06/09/2014

Thoughts without action are meaningless vapors.
It is our actions that give our thoughts power. I
can think "I need to eat" and if I do not then eat,
I will remain hungry. The thought was wasted.
Turn thoughts into actions to actually give them
meaning.

The importance of trusting yourself. 06/13/2014

When you trust yourself, you don't have to outsource it. You give yourself the autonomy to be interdependent or independent. You start to understand that you cannot expect someone else to give what they do not have for themselves, i.e. respect, generosity, appreciation etc.

X I A N 02/10/15

He said this time around he'd be better equipped
to deal with me—meaning the old me. This
person I am today was ready to love him—the
hymn from back then. Our roles had
reversed—except I wasn't unavailable. He had
hardened and I had softened.

A word from Guy Finley
04/10/16

"Byproducts of fear? Anything that causes fear, hatred or resentment is really a secret way in which we are invited to discover that these dark states are not adversarial but invitational, trying to invoke in us a realization that what we have been presented with is an opportunity to dive deeper into an order of ourselves in which this love that gave life to us can give us a completely new way to view problems as well as solve them." Perhaps one of the best run-on sentences ever.

She just doesn't get it
12/04/19

…well not even that, I'm talking about the abuse. I'm trying to speak gently here…we were abused.

-Yeah

I mean...we were sad, you had to know we were sad, we looked sad.

-Well, you looked scared. To me, you looked scared.

I think "and you were ok with that?" I say, "Well wasn't it your job to do something?"

-I did, isn't that why you went to live with your Dad?

*Unfortunately, usually when the parent doesn't get it, neither does the child.

A memory 01/14/20

I remember sometimes after my stepfather would rage against my sister and I? She would stand behind him giving us faces of sympathy but never actually stepping in and stopping anything from happening to us.

*Sometimes I have a hard time making sense of scenes from my past. Healthy reconciliation would require parties to be able to view events from alternate POVs and reach a fair consensus. It's not always possible, and I am learning to be okay with that.

A letter of gratitude 08/29/22

Dear God,

Thank you for the experience of my past choices
because without them, I wouldn't be who I am
today, ready to receive the fullness of this life.
Thank you for my beautiful daughter. The gift
through which I feel a pure love and have a
vessel to pour the best of me into. Thank you for
the future, which will be better than our past
provided we align ourselves to receive it. From
the little girl who once begged you to show her a
reason to live, thank you!

Jamaican Air Fryer Chickenback

Recipe provided by Coffy's Kitchen

2 lbs. chicken back
1 tsp. paprika
1 tsp. black pepper
1 1/2 tsp. garlic powder
1 tsp. salt
1/2 tsp. baking powder
1 1/2 tsp. all-purpose seasoning
1/2 cup all-purpose flour

Clean chicken backs by removing excess fat, and oysters. Scrub the chicken with fresh lemon or lime juice and vinegar.

Combine listed seasonings (minus baking powder,) setting aside about 1 1/2 tsp. Thoroughly coat well-cleaned chicken backs. For crispier backs, it is recommended that you cut the backs into smaller nugget-like pieces.

Put the flour in a seasoning bag with the remaining seasoning blend and the baking powder. Add the chicken pieces to the bag.

Shake all the pieces until well coated and shake off excess flour.

Let the chicken rest for about 10 minutes. Spray both sides with cooking oil spray.

Preheat the air-fryer to 350 degrees.

Lay the back pieces in a single layer in the air fry and let cook for about 10-13 minutes, flipping pieces and then cooking for another 5-7 minutes.

Drain grease and enjoy with preferred dipping sauce.

9 789358 315028